MARK MATLOCK

# WISDOM ON...
## MUSIC, MOVIES, AND TELEVISION

MARK MATLOCK

# WISDOM ON...
## MUSIC, MOVIES, AND TELEVISON

ZONDERVAN®

ZONDERVAN.com/
AUTHORTRACKER
follow your favorite authors

invert

youth
specialties

ZONDERVAN

*Wisdom On... Music, Movies, and Television*
Copyright 2008 by Mark Matlock

YS Youth Specialties is a trademark of YOUTHWORKS!, INCORPORATED
and is registered with the United States Patent and Trademark Office.

ISBN 978-0-310-27931-0

Cover design: *SharpSeven Design*
Interior design: *David Conn*

*Printed in the United States of America*

To my parents, Tom and Judi Matlock, who helped me discern the content of art and media and encouraged me to create some of my own.

TABLE OF CONTENTS

The first review I ever wrote for our website, planetwisdom.com, was for Star Wars Episode 1:The Phantom Menace. The response was so great that we started doing reviews regularly. But I soon found I didn't have enough time to keep up with every movie released. To cover as many films as possible, my good friend and fellow writer Chris Lyon started collaborating with me. Our conversations over the years about how to write and review media as Christ followers are the foundation of this book. Chris's ideas show up quite a bit here, and I'd like to thank him for letting me share them.

**ACKNOWLEDGMENTS**

# CHAPTER 1

## BEWITCHED, BOTHERED, AND BEWILDERED

**W**hen I was 10 years old, my favorite TV show was *Bewitched*. (Maybe you've seen the Will Ferrell movie remake.) The popular sitcom was about a witch who marries a mortal and tries to live without her magical powers. Needless to say, she doesn't always succeed.

The show had everything a 10-year-old could want—wacky characters, outrageous situations, plus hilarious and impressive (at the time) special effects. That's why I wanted to watch *Bewitched* more often than I wanted to watch any other show.

The problem was my parents didn't share my enthusiasm. In fact, they didn't like *Bewitched* at all. We attended a conservative Christian church that frowned on the show. My parents didn't know what to make of it, so they didn't let us watch it. Imagine what they'd have thought about *Harry Potter*!

And that's not all. My parents were also very particular about the music I listened to and the movies I watched. For example, I wasn't allowed to listen to rock stations on the radio. I wasn't allowed to see many movies that weren't made by Disney. My parents were careful to shield me from entertainment they considered to be morally objectionable, which usually meant things that portrayed sex or violence in a sleazy way.

Some of my parents' other rules weren't so clear-cut. In addition to *Bewitched*, I wasn't allowed to see *Escape from Witch Mountain*—a Disney movie. Even though there was nothing sleazy about either one of those shows, my parents considered them inappropriate for Christians to watch. I never really understood why. Their rules just seemed arbitrary to me.

As I got older, though, I noticed subtle changes in my parents' outlook on the media. They became less strict and gave my brothers and me more freedom in choosing the things we watched and listened to.

While they never wavered in their stance against morally or sexually objectionable material, they did ease up in their attitudes toward what they considered "proper" Christian media choices.

One day I asked them why their attitudes had changed. "We became better parents," they explained. "As we grew in our relationship with God, we became wiser."

Interesting isn't it? The more my parents' understanding of God's Word increased, the more freedom they gave us. That's the approach I want to take in this handy little guide. I want to help you apply God's wisdom to the media you watch, read, and listen to. In doing so, you may find more freedom in your life than ever before.

# CHAPTER 2
## THE POWER OF STORY

Most of the media we take in—whether it's a two-hour movie, a half-hour TV show, a four-minute music video, or a 30-second commercial—involves a story of some sort. There's a reason for that. Stories have a powerful impact on our lives. Stories stay with us long after the facts, figures, warnings, and advice have faded from our memories. Stories can shape our beliefs and influence the choices we make.

Consider this story that I heard from a friend of mine who's a police officer:

> A few weeks ago in a nearby city, a teenage girl sat down in a movie theater and felt something sharp poke through the seat of her jeans. She turned around to investigate, and she found a hypodermic needle sticking out of the seat. The needle had a label attached to it that read: YOU HAVE JUST BEEN INFECTED WITH HIV.

My friend told me that other cities in our area have reported similar incidents. However, the needles aren't always placed in movie theaters. Sometimes they're found in the cash drawers of ATMs or on the underside of gas pump handles.

Have you heard that story before?

How about the one in which a man meets a woman at a bar, takes her back to his hotel room, and then wakes up the next morning in a bathtub filled with ice—only to discover that one of his kidneys is missing?

Then there's the one in which gang members drive around at night in a car with its headlights turned off, daring people to flash their vehicle's headlights at them. And the unfortunate drivers who *do* are then targeted and killed as part of the gang's initiation.

All three of these stories are urban legends—made-up tales that are purported to be true. Urban legends spread like wildfire. Many people swear they really happened—usually to a friend of a friend of a friend—even after they're proved false. That's the power of stories.

I know the HIV needle incident never happened, but I still check my seat before I sit down in a movie theater! Stories can change the way we view the world and the way we make decisions—even if they aren't true.

In 2003, author Dan Brown grabbed the world's attention with a great story he'd concocted called *The DaVinci Code*. I don't read a lot of fiction (movies and comic books are more my style); but because so many students told me the story had shaken their faith, I decided to read it myself.

Once I started reading the book, I couldn't put it down. I'd tell myself, *Just one more chapter*, and then I'd read five more. The only thing that slowed me down was the weight of my tired eyelids. There's no denying that Dan Brown wrote a page-turner. In the process, though, he also threw out some pretty believable untruths that confused many people.

Since the book came out, Christians around the world have angrily wondered, *Who does this guy think he is? How can he claim Jesus was married and had children when there's no historical evidence to support it?* Dan Brown wasn't the first person to make such claims about Jesus, nor was he the best at defending his position. (I've read much better arguments for the theory that Jesus was married than those found in *The DaVinci Code*.) However, Mr. Brown was the first person to share this theory within the context of a story. That's why his book had such an impact.

Stories are powerful communication tools. The wise student will seek to understand their power so as not to be deceived by them.

And that's the purpose of this book: To help you understand how media works so you can make informed decisions about your viewing and listening habits. If you know how to process the stories you encounter, then you'll better understand how they impact your relationship with God and the good life you want to live.

# CHAPTER 3
## GOD MADE US CREATIVE

**O**ur attraction to stories—and the creativity that inspires them—comes naturally. After all, God is the Creator of everything that exists, and we were made to love him and his nature. The first five words of the Bible are "In the beginning God created." What's more, the fact that we're made in God's likeness means we share his characteristics. If God is creative, then you and I are creative, too.

In the Garden of Eden, God commanded Adam and Eve to "fill the earth and subdue it" (Genesis 1:28). In other words, we're called to master what God has made. God invites us to be "cocreators" with him. First, he made the basics: Colors, natural resources (such as trees, rocks, and the elements we learn about in chemistry), and natural order (including the laws of physics and the orderly systems of the human body). He then gave us the freedom to use the things he made in order to exercise our own creativity.

As a result, we've learned to manipulate materials to make houses, to master the human body and optimize our health, to unleash the power of nuclear elements, and to harness the smallest fluctuation in an electron to create shelves full of electronic gadgetry. We also have the ability to make art and music and to tell stories.

That creative ability of ours is a double-edged sword, though. One of the consequences of sin is that we have the ability to corrupt God's creation with our own creative acts. We discovered the power of the atom...and then we used it in a destructive way to kill people. We harnessed energy to create the combustible engine...and then we made machines that destroyed the beauty of the environment and led to the extinction of God's creatures.

Likewise, our works of imagination can corrupt what God has made. As we seek wisdom regarding music, television, and movies, that potential for corruption must be constantly in our thoughts. We must ask ourselves: *Does the creative work make God's character known or does it ignore or corrupt what God calls "good"?*

# CHAPTER 4

## WHY DO CHRISTIANS FUSS ABOUT THE MEDIA?

I attended public schools from kindergarten through high school. But when the time came for me to go to college, I chose Biola University, a private Christian school. As part of my enrollment, I had to sign a document stating I wouldn't participate in dancing while I was a student at Biola. If you've ever seen me dance, then you'd probably assume the restriction was for the sake of the other students—but everyone had to sign it. You had to give up dancing in order to attend Biola.

Since dancing wasn't something I enjoyed, signing the agreement was easy for me. For other students, however, it was much more difficult. And it made me ask the question: *Is dancing so wrong that it should be banned?*

The movie *Footloose* came out a few years prior to my stint at Biola. It's about a churched community that pro-

hibits dancing and a group of teenagers who work to change the adults'
minds. The students even use Scripture
to show that King David danced before the Lord. Eventually, the teenagers
are allowed to dance (just in time for
prom!); and coincidentally, so were the
Biola students.

During my freshman year, the
50-some-year-old dancing prohibition
was lifted. And that change begged a
new question: *Why? Did the trustees of
the university suddenly adopt a looser
interpretation of appropriate Christian
behavior? Were they being more true to
their understanding of Scripture?* That
question was the subject of much conversation at school.

Almost 15 years after I graduated
from Biola, I hosted an alumni reunion
at my home in Texas. Many of the people who attended are much older than
I am. And as we talked, they shared

how they also weren't allowed to play cards or go to the movies when they were Biola students. No games of go fish, hearts, or gin rummy—and definitely no poker!

Today most Christians don't think twice about going to movies or playing cards. So what's changed? People's attitudes and preconceptions. Once upon a time, movies and dances were considered unsavory activities. Right or wrong, they were closely associated with non-Christian behavior. As time marched on and other generations emerged, those forms of entertainment eventually became less associated with evil.

During the more restrictive periods of time, there were those who helped change people's minds by demonstrating that one could have a dynamic relationship with Christ while still watching movies and playing cards and—gasp!—dancing. Sometimes those people were accused of "leading others astray." But they helped many people live more truthfully by showing that righteousness could coexist with activities that were once considered damaging to the Christian faith.

Jesus often challenged established rules and restrictions. He healed on the Sabbath, and he didn't require his disciples to follow all of the Jewish cleansing rituals. These kinds of decisions caused controversy, to say the least. Scripture says Jesus "came eating and drinking" and was a friend of sinners. His enemies accused him of being a drunkard and a glutton (See Matthew 11:19 and Luke 7:34).

Yet the Bible also makes it clear that Jesus never sinned. He didn't let conventional wisdom determine what was and wasn't off-limits for him. Jesus proved that certain "unacceptable" things could be done by righteous people.

A missionary shared a story about his work among a group of people in Latin America. He said the first-generation Christians in that region strongly objected to using certain musical instruments—particularly the marimba—during worship. They associated those sounds with their lives as nonbelievers and hearing them reminded the people of a life they didn't want to relive—a life before they knew Jesus, before they had hope.

However, as new generations grew up in that Latin American church, they saw no connection between musical instruments and godless living. So they incorporated those sounds into the worship service.

For the first time in our history as Christians in America, the church is embracing art forms such as dance, drama, film, and a wide variety of music. You're blessed to live during this special time. In order to fully appreciate that blessing, though, you need to understand how we got to this point.

# CHAPTER 5

## HOW SHOULD CHRISTIANS
## THINK ABOUT MEDIA?

Scripture teaches that believers have always had to be discerning when it comes to the things people create. In the Old and New Testaments, artisans were often involved in creating objects of worship. They built ornate temples so people could come together and worship false gods. They also forged statues of those gods—called "idols"—so people could worship them in their homes.

Rather than honor the true living God, the artists used their creative skills to glorify imaginary deities. It's likely that some of the pieces they created were awe-inspiring—perhaps even masterpieces. But they violated the first and second commandments:

> "You shall have no other gods before me. You shall not make for yourself an idol in the form of anything in heaven above or on the earth beneath or in the waters below. You

shall not bow down to them or worship them." (Exodus 20:3-5)

One of the best-known examples of idolatrous art can be found in Daniel 3. King Nebuchadnezzar of Babylon ordered the construction of a golden statue that was 90 feet tall and 9 feet wide. Then he summoned all of the leaders in the region to attend the unveiling ceremony. To guarantee a positive reaction to his creation, Nebby decreed that when he gave the signal, everyone had to fall down and worship the statue. Those who didn't, he warned, would be thrown into a furnace and burned to death.

Among the invited guests were three Israelites: Shadrach, Meshach, and Abednego. They worshipped the one true living God, which meant they couldn't bow down to an idol. So when the signal was given, Shadrach, Meshach, and Abednego stood their ground. And true to his word, the king had the men thrown into the furnace. You probably know how the story goes from there: God protected them from the flames, and King Neb was so impressed by their Divine rescue that he declared the God of Israel to be the only God.

But that's not the point I want to make here. You see, Shadrach, Meshach, and Abednego could have just skipped the whole dedication ceremony. They could have refused to have anything to do with the creative work of idol worshippers. Their fate would have been the same either way.

However, Shadrach and his friends chose to attend the ceremony because they were active members of the government. They probably admired the artistic aspects of the statue and the craftsmanship that went into making it. Yet while the three men chose not to honor the creative work with their lives (by bowing down to it), they didn't ignore it or boycott it, either.

What's more, earlier in the book of Daniel we learn that Shadrach, Meshach, and Abednego had been schooled in the Babylonian language and literature (Daniel 1:3-4). Because the young men excelled in those areas, the king placed them in positions of influence and authority where they were able to help others learn about God and come to know him.

That should also be our goal in learning about our own culture. Movies, television, and music (along with art and literature) reveal the heart and soul of who we are as people. When we understand the culture we live in, we can apply that knowledge as we introduce others to God. The more we know about what people are really connecting with, the better prepared we'll be to introduce God in a context they can relate to.

# CHAPTER 6

## WHY DO PEOPLE, WATCH, READ, AND LISTEN?

W hy do you turn on the TV? Why do you listen to music? Why do you go to movies? They're all basic questions, but ones we don't consider very often.

Sometimes music is just background noise for me—a silence filler. I'm not even aware of what's playing. Other times I listen to enjoy a favorite song or artist...and maybe do a little karaoke in front of the mirror. But that's beside the point. The point is, sometimes my mind is engaged when I listen to music and sometimes it isn't.

Television is a different story. Unless I'm watching a show that's teaching me something (Alton Brown showing me how to cook squid on the Food Network, for example), I usually just veg out in front of the tube. The only other exception is when my family and I watch *American Idol* together. In that case, we have a good time sharing a show as a family.

I don't go to movies like I used to. Our Web site (planetwisdom.com) does on-line movie reviews, so we receive passes to see films before they're officially released. But in those situations, going to movies is work. I have to think about what I'm watching so I can write an article about it or approve an article written by someone else. It feels like an obligation. Most people, though, go to movies to have a good time.

Here are some other reasons you might go to a movie, turn on the TV, or listen to music. Circle any that describe your motives or write in some of your own reasons.

To escape reality

To learn

To stay current on the latest things

To laugh

To be challenged emotionally and intellectually

To have something to do

To spend time with friends

To be inspired

To appreciate the art of another person

Other _____

The way we use our time matters. We have only so much of it, so we want to make sure that when we spend time reading, watching, or listening, we're making the most of it. To do that, we need the skill of discernment.

*Discernment* is the ability to judge well—in this case it's the ability to determine whether or not something is worth our time.

# CHAPTER 7
## LEARN TO DISCERN

Understanding the motives behind your media habits gives you a foundation for evaluating those habits. We don't have space in this book to debate the pros and cons of every possible motive. But we can explore some key biblical principles that shed some light on the topic.

The common denominator among all of the motives on our list is pleasure. The desire for pleasure is the reason we listen to music, plop down in front of the tube, or go see a movie. And there's nothing wrong with that. Pleasure is a great thing—in moderation. Proverbs 21:17 warns,

> He who loves pleasure will become poor; whoever loves wine and oil will never be rich.

If we consume media too often, then we rob ourselves of productivity. Many studies show that sitting in front of the television for long periods of time leads to obesity and negatively impacts school performance. Recent studies have also linked television viewing to an increased likelihood of ADD and Alzheimer's.

In addition to the physical effects, there are also mental and spiritual effects to consider. Most media consumption is passive: We sit and watch (or listen). Period. We disengage our brains and absorb what's in front of us. That's a problem for Christians who are called to imitate Christ and make a difference in the world. In order to make a difference, our minds need to be fully engaged.

Consider Paul's words to the Christians in Corinth:

> I beg you that when I come I may not have to be as bold as I expect to be

toward some people who think that we live by the standards of this world. For though we live in the world, we do not wage war as the world does. The weapons we fight with are not the weapons of the world. On the contrary, they have divine power to demolish strongholds. We demolish arguments and every pretension that sets itself up against the knowledge of God, and we take captive every thought to make it obedient to Christ. (2 Corinthians 10:2-5)

With our minds engaged, we can take from this passage three nuggets of wisdom to apply to our media habits.

### 1. WE AREN'T FIGHTING PEOPLE.
As Christians, we're not called to fight Marilyn Manson, Paris Hilton, Quentin Tarantino, or any other person in the entertainment industry. God loves those people and so should we.

When *The DaVinci Code* came out, I wasn't mad at Dan Brown or Ron Howard for writing the book and making the movie. They didn't have a problem with the story they were telling. I want Dan and Ron to recognize the truth about Jesus and come to know him. Attacking them won't make that happen. We get off track when we personalize our objections to the media—when we attack people instead of debating the ideas they hold.

The world that's mentioned in 2 Corinthians 10 doesn't refer to the people of this planet. Instead, it refers to the faulty system of beliefs that guides the way many people live. As Christians we're fighting against a bad way of thinking—not against the people who think that way.

## 2. WE HAVE A RESPONSIBILITY TO TAKE ISSUE WITH BAD IDEAS.

Paul encourages Christians to "be transformed by the renewing of your mind" (Romans 12:2). Genuine change happens when we get rid of ideas that destroy our lives and replace them with the truth and wisdom God has revealed to us. Later in this book we'll take a look at some specific bad ideas and explore ways to respond to them.

## 3. WE'RE CALLED TO TAKE OUR THOUGHTS CAPTIVE TO THE OBEDIENCE OF CHRIST.

We can't put our brains on autopilot as we enjoy media. All of our thoughts must be taken to Christ to see how they measure up. Some of those thoughts will survive; many will be exposed as lies. That's discernment in action—learning how to judge what's good by the standard of Christ.

## SELF-EVALUATION: WHAT ARE MY CURRENT LIMITS?

Before you jump into the next section that talks about deciding what's worth watching, listening to, and reading, ask yourself the following questions:

· How do I currently decide if a movie is okay for me to watch in the theater? On DVD? On TV? While at a friend's house?

· Do I ever tell myself "no" when it comes to media choices—even if nobody has told me I can't read, watch, or listen to something?

· What movies, TV shows, games, or music have I chosen to avoid? Why?

· Should the same media standards apply to all Christians?

Or is it possible that a movie that's okay for another Christian to watch may not be okay for me to see?

· Who has the right to tell me I can't watch, listen to, or read something—even if I believe it would be okay for me?

# CHAPTER 8

## YOUR MEDIA MATTERS:
## ASKING YOURSELF THE
## HARD QUESTIONS

**L**et's boil all this thinking down into some practical questions we can ask ourselves about the media we devour. I use the word *devour* because that's how most people interact with media in our world today. There are just so many songs, TV shows, books, comics, and films available to us that many people consume them nonstop and with very little thought beforehand—and very little thought after it's been downloaded into the hard drives of their brains.

The questions we should all be asking ourselves about media come in two stages. The first involves preplanning: *Should I watch/listen to/read/look at this media?* The second question comes after the choice has been made to ingest the stories and ideas in a movie, CD, or book: *How should I think about what I just took into my mind?*

Let's start with the first one.

## BIG QUESTION: SHOULD I WATCH, LISTEN TO, OR LOOK AT THIS?

Over the years I've received hundreds of questions from Christian students asking which media is okay for them to take in and which should be prohibited. The questions arrive in emails to our planetwisdom.com Web site and to my media column for *Ignite Your Faith* magazine (formerly *Campus Life*):

"Should Christians read the *Harry Potter* books and watch the movies?"

"Should Christians listen to hip-hop and rap music?"

"What about music with swearing in it?"

"Should believers watch crude comedy films? How about violent horror movies like the *Hostel* series or bloody action films like *300*?"

"Should Christians play first-person shooter video games?"

"What do you think of shows like *My Name Is Earl, Ugly Betty,* and *American Idol?*"

In my answers, I do try to respond to a question about a particular show, but I also try to make a bigger point: When it comes to making media choices, what impact does the music, book, or TV show make on you and on your relationship with God? Are you being honest with yourself about why you want to watch or listen to it?

Many students (and parents) just want some Christian leader or organization to make a list of media that's okay to consume so they can take it in without having to think about it for themselves. They want someone to make their watching/listening/playing rules for them so they don't have to make the hard choices. In short, they want what we call *legalism.*

Of course, *they* wouldn't call it that because we all think of legalism as a bad thing. But honestly, living under legalism can make life a lot easier. You never have to decide things for yourself. If a show's not on "the list," then it's bad. If it *is* on the list, then it's safe to consume—even if your heart tells you otherwise.

One way to describe legalism is the creation of rules "built onto" God's Word to "protect" people from getting too close to sin. Earlier in the book, I talked about how Christians once made rules against dancing. They did this because they noticed how certain kinds of dances led students to cross boundaries of physical intimacy, which made it easier to go even further sexually once a couple was alone. Their reasoning was, "If we stop the dancing, then maybe it'll take longer for teenagers to get that close and sensual with each other in private."

One problem with legalism is that it doesn't work. Rules may or may not be effective in standing in the way of sinful choices. But rules don't change sinful hearts. Teenagers who make the choice to get sexual with each other won't be stopped by not going to dances. And they won't be stopped by not seeing movies rated R for "strong sexuality" or by not listening to sexually explicit rap music.

Does that mean we should all allow ourselves to consume everything the media has to offer? Should parents encourage their teenagers to participate in provocative dancing since it's not specifically forbidden in the Bible? Should I not make anything in the world of media off-limits to myself? Of course not!

As Christians, we have a responsibility to ask ourselves tougher questions than "Is this on the nice or naughty list?" Our first priority is to follow Jesus. In order to do that, we must eliminate everything in our lives that gets in the way of walking the path he's called us to. If you really want to make wise media choices, then here's what you need:

## A SUBMISSIVE SPIRIT

Forget about me or your youth leader or your pastor or even your parents for a minute. Have you made the choice in your head that the God of the universe has the right to tell you what to watch, listen to, and look at? Have you decided that God's Word is the final word in your life? Do you take the Bible as the ultimate authority on every issue you face, even down to whether or not you'll watch a rerun of *Scrubs*?

## A RUTHLESS SELF-HONESTY

David wrote in Psalm 51:6 that God really wants us to have truth in the "inner parts." Are you willing to look yourself in the eye and be honest about your motives for wanting to see a show or listen to a CD? Can you own the truth about why you "have to" catch a particular movie or how a certain style of music makes you feel?

## A SENSITIVITY TO THE HOLY SPIRIT

The Bible teaches that all believers receive God's Spirit when they trust in Jesus for their salvation. One of the Holy Spirit's jobs is to influence us in the direction that God is leading us, even as it relates to our media choices. Are you aware of the Holy Spirit's prompting when it comes to the video games you play or the books you read or the Web sites you visit?

### SELF-EVALUATION: AM I READY TO MAKE MY OWN MEDIA DECISIONS?
For each question below, circle the answer that best represents you.

## DO I HAVE A SUBMISSIVE SPIRIT?

· Yes, I accept that God has the right to tell me what to do and that he's given certain people authority in my life. I follow that direction without a problem most of the time.

· While I accept that God is the ultimate authority in my life and that he's given authority to my parents, I really struggle to obey his—and their—instructions.

· I'm okay with God as my authority, but I don't believe my parents have the right to tell me what to do.

· I'm in charge of me. Period. I don't give anyone the absolute right to tell me what to do or not to do.

**AM I ABLE TO BE BRUTALLY HONEST WITH MYSELF ABOUT MY TRUE MOTIVES, DESIRES, AND RESPONSES WHEN IT COMES TO THE MEDIA?**

· I think so. I regularly think through my reasons for wanting to do things. I'm willing to consider that my motives might be selfish or sinful.

· I'm not sure. If I'm really good at lying to myself, then how would I know?

· I don't think so. I can make any unwise choice sound noble or good if I really want to.

**AM I SENSITIVE TO THE LEADING OF THE HOLY SPIRIT IN MY LIFE?**

· I sometimes ask God to direct my life, and I know his Spirit is at work in me to do just that.

· Not really. I don't pray much, and I've never asked God to help me make wise choices through the leading of his Spirit.

· I don't even know what that means.

If you're on board in these three areas, then I believe you have what you need to begin deciding for yourself (with God's leading) what media you should allow into your head and heart. You're ready to start letting go of other people's lists of what's okay for you to watch and listen to and read.

If you're looking for a place to start, try answering some questions to get you thinking about how to rule in or rule out various media choices.

## WHAT DO MY PARENTS SAY?

Remember our earlier discussion about having a submissive spirit? If you're still living at home and under your parents' authority, then the Bible makes it crystal clear that you have a responsibility to obey and honor them, no matter what.

> Children, obey your parents in the Lord, for this is right. "Honor your father and mother"—which is the first commandment with a promise—"that it may go well with you and that you may enjoy long life on the earth." (Ephesians 6:1-3)

You simply cannot justify before God a choice to consume any media that your parents have restricted. Period. It's always wrong to do so.

It may seem unfair when your mom or dad says no to a movie, TV show, or video game—especially if your Christian friends are all enjoying it with their parents' blessings. You may not be convinced that your parents' decision—or even their motive for making that decision—is right. It's true that some parents get on power trips and say no just because they can. It's also true that some parents make decisions out of fear or a legalistic mindset.

But you have to keep three things in mind if you're serious about following Jesus.

**FIRST, GOD DIRECTS YOUR LIFE THROUGH YOUR PARENTS' AUTHORITY**—even if it seems like they're wrong, selfish, or confused. Ephesians 6:1-3 emphasizes that God uses parental authority to keep your life moving in the direction he wants it to go. Sometimes it takes blind faith to believe that's true, but the God you're putting your faith in is trustworthy.

**SECOND, YOUR PARENTS OFTEN DO KNOW BETTER THAN YOU DO.** The vast majority of Christian adults I know—who all survived their teen years—now say they're really glad their mom and dad laid down the law on certain issues. At the time, they hated it. But now they see the wisdom in their parents' choices. Others who made foolish and destructive choices as teenagers sometimes wonder, *Where were my parents when I was going through all of that? Why didn't they step in and tell me to stop?*

What did the writer of Proverbs say about parental instruction?

> The eye that mocks a father, that scorns obedience to a mother, will be pecked out by the ravens of the valley, will be eaten by the vultures. (Proverbs 30:17)

Okay, let's try something a little less gross and a little more helpful:

My son, keep your father's commands and do not forsake your mother's teaching. Bind them upon your heart forever; fasten them around your neck. When you walk, they will guide you; when you sleep, they will watch over you; when you awake, they will speak to you. (Proverbs 6:20-22)

God designed the family to work this way: Parents pass on their hard-earned wisdom to their children. Wise kids hold onto that wisdom and put it into practice—even when they don't exactly understand how their mom and dad could be right about a specific thing. But those children who refuse to be guided and directed by their parents tend to become lifelong fools:

A fool spurns his father's discipline, but whoever heeds correction shows prudence. (Proverbs 15:5)

A *fool* is a person who makes unwise choices throughout his life. In our current age, that would include choices about what media he sticks in his cranium. Your parents can help you to avoid such a fate.

As you get older, your parents will (hopefully) begin to give you more freedom in choosing what media you consume. If you've earned their trust by making wise choices in other areas of your life, then you'll make it easier for them to trust you to think through your options for movies, music, books, and video games.

Here's a great idea: Ask your parents for their advice. Notice how I said "advice." I'm not suggesting you practice legalism by having your parents tell you what to watch for the rest of your life. But I am suggesting that when they give you a choice, you should occasionally ask them what they believe the pros and cons are before you choose.

Remember, your mom and dad know you better than most people do. They've been living with you and watching out for you for a long time. Therefore, your parents' perspective is usually worth listening to.

**THIRD, IF YOUR PARENTS ARE EXTREMELY RESTRICTIVE ABOUT YOUR MEDIA CHOICES, THEN JUST HOLD ON.** You'll be living on your own in a few years. And in our digital age, every movie, TV show, and other kind of media will still be available to watch or listen to on the very day you move out of your folks' house. So in the meantime, you don't need to dishonor them with your attempts to avoid missing out on what you really want to see. Just wait awhile. If you still want to watch that same movie or TV show when you're 18 or 21 or 25 years old, then you'll be better able to decide for yourself whether or not it's a good idea.

## SELF-EVALUATION: DO I FOLLOW MY PARENTS' DIRECTION ABOUT WHAT MEDIA TO CONSUME?

· Have you ever disobeyed your parents' directions about what you could watch, listen to, or play?

· If so, did you confess it to them and try to make it right?

· Do you believe God directs your life through the authority of your parents?

· Do you ever ask your parents for advice about tough decisions? About media decisions?

· Do you feel as though you have to keep your media choices a secret from your parents?

> · Would they be surprised (or disappointed) if they knew about some of the things you watch, listen to, or read?

## WILL CONSUMING THIS MEDIA MAKE IT EASIER FOR ME TO SIN?

A popular motto in the early Christian church was "All things are permissible." Believers were reveling in God's grace and the freedom it offered from the system of Jewish laws and the restrictive rules of many other religions.

However, the apostle Paul made it clear that freedom was *not* about giddily doing whatever comes naturally to us. Look at what he said to one group of Christians while correcting some of their choices:

"Everything is permissible"—but not everything is beneficial. "Everything is permissible"—but not everything is constructive. (1 Corinthians 10:23)

It's much easier to choose to avoid certain movies or songs because they're "not okay for Christians" than it is to choose to avoid them just because they're not helpful or constructive in your quest to live like Jesus.

## WILL THIS MEDIA CHOICE CAUSE ME TO STRUGGLE WITH FEAR?

Do you know which command is delivered most often in the New Testament? It's "Do not be afraid" or "Fear not." God wants us to move beyond our fears and learn to trust him to provide for us and to protect us. Movies, TV shows, and games that interfere with that process should be considered unwise choices.

It's one thing to watch movies or TV shows that make us jump in our seats or momentarily creep us out. They can provide a fun adrenaline rush. It's the stories that leave us with a lingering sense of fear hours after they're over that should make us question the wisdom of watching them.

I can't tell you how many emails we received from students after the first movie in *The Ring* series came out. Apparently, that story really got inside people's heads. Days later, they still felt a little unhinged by that creepy, black-haired girl coming out of the TV. Our reviewer on PlanetWisdom even admitted to listening all night long for the TV to turn itself on after watching that movie.

Was it a sin to watch *The Ring*? I don't believe so. Is it a sin to feel fearful? No. Fear is a normal human emotion. Based on the Bible's commands, though, we can say it's a sin to live in fear. Paul told Timothy that a "spirit of timidity" or fear is not something that comes from God (2 Timothy 1:7). As people who are learning to trust God, it's our job to learn to get fear out of our lives.

So where does that leave us in deciding whether or not to watch movies like *The Ring*? Remember our earlier guidelines. Ask yourself, *Am I being submissive to God? Am I willing to pass up a chance to watch a film if it's likely to lead my heart in the wrong direction? Am I being honest with myself about my probable response to this kind of story? Am I open to allowing God's Holy Spirit to direct my choice?*

After you've thoughtfully considered those questions, make your choice. I know people who watch movies like *The Ring* and then fall asleep two minutes later and never think about them again. Movies don't affect them on any fear level.

On the other hand, I also know plenty of people who can't stop being afraid long after the credits have rolled. If someone like that is honest with himself about a film that may stir up a lot of fearful feelings, then the question he must answer is, *Why go? How will that media choice be beneficial in trying to follow Jesus' path?*

Solomon wrote that learning to make wise choices can help us overcome fear in our hearts and minds:

> My son, preserve sound judgment and discernment, do not let them out of your sight...[Then] when you lie down, you will not be afraid; when you lie down, your sleep will be sweet. Have no fear of sudden disaster or of the ruin that overtakes the wicked, for the Lord will be your

confidence and will keep your foot from being snared. (Proverbs 3:21, 24-26)

I believe this passage could also be applied to using good judgment about the media we allow into our thoughts.

Use God's wisdom to help you make wise choices regarding stories that may leave you with lingering fear.

## SELF-EVALUATION: DO I CONSIDER THE "FEAR FACTOR" WHEN I MAKE MEDIA CHOICES?

· Has a movie, TV show, or book ever caused you to struggle with fear—even after you finished it? If so, list a few examples.

· Some people claim to enjoy being scared by a story. Why?

· Do you believe there's a difference between the rush of being scared during a story and still feeling scared by it days later?

· Why doesn't God want us to be afraid?

· Have you ever skipped a movie, television show, or some other media because you knew it would cause you to struggle with fear? If not, then would you ever do so?

## WILL THIS MEDIA CHOICE CAUSE ME TO STRUGGLE WITH SEXUALLY IMMORAL THOUGHTS?

Answering this question requires you to be really honest with yourself about your motives for seeing a film, watching a music video, or returning to a TV show week after week.

When I was a teenager, I realized that not everyone has the same response to media's sexual content that many teenage boys do. Older people and girls would talk about how much they liked a movie or a TV show without ever mentioning the fact that it contained some intense sex scenes or some extremely attractive women wearing very little clothing. It's sometimes difficult, especially for teenage guys, to think about those movies without focusing on those moments or images—no matter how brief the scenes were.

That's where personal responsibility before God comes in. If you know a movie is likely to contain impure sexual content that you'll have trouble getting out of your head afterward, then consider whether the experience of seeing the film (or watching the show or listening to the song) is worth the resulting struggle with lustful thoughts.

In Matthew 5:28, Jesus makes it clear that lusting after someone you're not married to is wrong. Period. He said it's like committing adultery in your heart. And Paul warns that God's standard for Christians is higher than his standard for non-Christians. In other words, as God's people we have no room in our lives for even a *little bit* of impurity.

> But among you there must not be even a hint of sexual immorality, or of any kind of impurity, or of greed, because these are improper for God's holy people. (Ephesians 5:3)

Part of our job as followers of Jesus is to do fatal violence to our sin nature. That includes our tendency toward sexual sin.

> Put to death, therefore, whatever belongs to your earthly nature: sexual immorality, impurity, lust, evil

desires and greed, which is idolatry. Because of these, the wrath of God is coming. (Colossians 3:5-6)

I'm not suggesting it's wrong to have sexual desires. God created us as sexual beings. But it is wrong, according to God's Word, to indulge those sexual desires either in our minds (lusting) or with our bodies (having sex outside of marriage). So you have to ask yourself, *How much harder will it be to kill my old-nature tendency to indulge in immoral sexual thoughts if I watch this movie or TV show?*

I know students who've set limits for what they'll allow themselves to watch, even though their parents give them permission to watch a particular film or TV show. I admire that. They understand that wise media choices aren't about what someone will *let* them watch; they're about what will help or hurt them in their walk with Jesus.

Solomon warned his young male readers that sexual sin starts with the path one chooses. He describes watching a foolish young man who made the mistake of taking the route nearest to temptation:

> At the window of my house I looked out through the lattice. I saw among the simple, I noticed among the young men, a youth who lacked judgment. He was going down the street near her corner, walking along in the direction of her house at twilight, as the day was fading, as the dark of night set in. Then out came a woman to meet him, dressed like a prostitute and with crafty intent. (Proverbs 7:6-10)

The path to sexual sin always starts with the mind. The first temptation is to indulge ourselves in what we look at, to get too close to things we shouldn't be near, to let our curiosity get the better of us. In today's world, those issues often involve media choices. *What Web sites will I visit? What shows will I watch? What songs will I allow to become the soundtrack of my week?*

*Will this media choice cause me to struggle with sexually immoral thoughts?* This question is difficult to answer partly because people respond to things in different ways. It takes a lot of courage to say, "I'm not going to watch this," when your good friends (who are also good Christians) don't seem to have a problem with it. Remember, though, *you're* the one who must take the responsibility for your media consumption.

King David didn't have wireless broadband Internet access at his palace, but it would be great to write his words on a sticky note and attach it to your computer monitor or TV: "I will set before my eyes no vile thing" (Psalm 101:3).

And guys, you could put these words of Job on a second sticky note: "I made a covenant with my eyes not to look lustfully at a girl" (Job 31:1).

While we've talked about this issue mainly from a guy's perspective, the same thing applies to girls. Many teenage girls openly lust after guys—or get fixated on a male celebrity and make him their "boyfriend" in their hearts. If those fixations cross over into immoral sexual thoughts, then a girl has to be honest with herself about whether watching that guy's TV shows and movies—or constantly reading about him in magazines—is worth the battle for her heart's purity.

Can you see how much easier it would be to just take a legalistic approach to media and rely on someone else to make these choices for you? You and I live in a media-saturated culture. So for us, walking with God means making hard, honest choices about which media gets into our heads and hearts. Taking in a movie, song, or book with content that makes us struggle with sexual sin is *not* worth the entertainment it provides.

**SELF-EVALUATION: DO I CONSIDER SEXUAL TEMPTATION WHEN I MAKE MY MEDIA CHOICES?**

· Think of some movies, TV shows, or other media that have caused you to wrestle with immoral thoughts. What kinds of content cause you the most trouble in that area?

· Do you ever ingest movies, TV, or other media because you want to fuel those thoughts?

· Do you ever avoid movies, TV, or other media because you don't want to wrestle with sexual sin?

· Why do you believe sexual purity is such a big deal to God?

· Do you ever struggle with the idea that other Christians are taking in movies or TV shows that you'd like to see but you're afraid they'd lead your mind in the wrong direction?

· Do your friends care about these issues, or do they just watch whatever they want without thinking about it?

## WILL THIS MEDIA CHOICE CAUSE ME TO STRUGGLE WITH ANGER?

More studies are confirming that exposure to media violence has a definite impact on how our brains work—especially teenage brains. In a 2006 study conducted by the Indiana University School of Medicine, researchers hooked up 44 adolescents to MRI machines that map brain activity. They had the students play fast-paced video games with half the group playing something violent and the other half playing something nonviolent.

The results clearly showed that those who played the violent games had significantly different responses in two parts of their brains. They experienced *more* activity in a region associated with "emotional arousal." In other words, they got seriously hyped up. But they experienced *less* activity in a brain region associated with self-control. As a result, the violent-video-game players tended to be more worked up and less inhibited than other people.

Am I saying it's wrong to play violent video games? Not necessarily. Am I saying it's wrong to have your brain pumping with emotions and your inhibitions lowered? Not always. And let me say for the record that I'm not associating video-game playing with school shootings or other teenage violence, either. What I *am* saying is that you and I need to take responsibility before God for controlling our anger.

Remember Paul's violent imagery about killing off our earthly nature? Look at what else he said Jesus followers should assassinate:

> But now you must rid yourselves of all such things as these: anger, rage, malice, slander, and filthy language from your lips. (Colossians 3:8)

As Christians it's our job to kill our anger, rage (out-of-control anger), malice (anger that makes us want to hurt someone), slander (hurting someone's reputation out of anger), and filthy words (the kind we often blurt out in anger).

We're back to that brutal self-honesty again. Think about your media diet. Are some of the things on the menu likely to stir up feelings of anger? If so, then those choices won't help you live more like Jesus. In fact, that music, those games, and those movies are only going to get in the way.

You and I both know people who seem to thrive on anger. It's as if they believe they need anger in order to stay energized and focused. Therefore, anger is involved in almost all of their choices. And when their anger begins to wear off, they start to feel weak and lost.

I know people like that who use music, especially, to get their anger back. Generally speaking, it's not the latest Ashlee Simpson CD that does it for them. They need hard, fast, and aggressive rock, thrash, punk, metal, or rap music to fuel their rage. Does that mean those styles of music are wrong? Not at all. Not unless they fuel your rage and you're a person who's trying to live like Jesus. Then they're wrong for you.

If God tells you to kill your anger, then are you willing to submit to that by avoiding media that builds your anger? Can you be honest with yourself about what makes you mad? Are you listening for God's Spirit to steer you away from anger-churning video games?

*Wait a minute, some of you may be saying. It's true that some movies, music, or games get me a little worked up, but that's not a big deal. Feeling angry is a normal human emotion.* I agree. It's extremely normal. And being angry is not a sin. Paul made that clear by repeating King David's teaching from Psalm 4:4: "In your anger, do not sin."

But in the next breath, Paul also made it clear that anger is spiritually dangerous: "Do not let the sun go down while you are still angry, and do not give the devil a foothold" (Ephesians 4:26-27). He implies that by holding on to anger—by keeping it alive inside of us—we give our spiritual enemy a way to influence our lives. We open the door to demonic involvement in our daily activities. Any entertainment that tends to stir up our anger isn't worth the price of letting our enemy—who wants to destroy us—"behind the lines," so to speak.

*Wait a minute,* others may be saying. *Jesus got angry. Paul and James and Peter all sound angry in some of their writing. Those Old Testament prophets got royally ticked off too, right?* Right, they did. For the sake of God's honor and glory, they all got mad and expressed God's outrage. And there's a place for that kind of emotion in our lives. A good story that reveals human injustice can—and maybe should—make us angry in defense of the victims of real wrongdoing.

But, being real again for a minute, that's not the anger most of us struggle with on a daily basis. Instead, we wrestle with human anger. And James wrote in his New Testament book of wisdom, "Man's anger does not bring about the righteous life that God desires" (James 1:20).

Solomon agreed that ramping up your anger makes everything in life harder: "For as churning the milk produces butter, and as twisting the nose produces blood, so stirring up anger produces strife" (Proverbs 30:33).

Notice that I'm not making a rule that says you can't listen to angry music or watch revenge movies or play first-person shooter games. I'm saying that if you're serious about obeying God, then you've got to ask yourself if any of those things (or others) tend to stir up your anger and make it harder for you to let it go. If so, then none of them is worth what that entertainment is costing you.

### SELF-EVALUATION: WHAT PART DOES ANGER PLAY IN YOUR MEDIA CHOICES?

· Do you tend to get angry easily? Do you like feeling angry?

· Do you see anger being a problem in your life?

· Why is human anger such a big deal to God?

· What's the problem with being controlled by anger?

· Do any of the media choices that you consume stir up your anger? List a few examples.

> · What would it cost you to give up some of the movies, games, or TV shows that fuel your anger?
>
> · What will it cost you to keep consuming them?

## HOW MUCH IS ENOUGH?

Someone once told me he thought it would be better for a person to watch *Hostel 2* once and then not watch anything else for a whole week than to watch 50 hours of the Disney Channel in a week. And he wasn't talking about whether it was "okay" to watch either one. (He'd actually prefer that no one watch *Hostel 2*.) He was talking about the impact of gorging ourselves on electronic media.

I'm not sure I completely agree with him, but I get what he's saying. Too much electronic media can have a negative impact on our lives that goes way beyond the impact of one destructive 90-minute film.

Forty years ago, electronic media choices were slim. There was radio, three television networks (and PBS), the record player, and maybe a few movie theaters in town. That was about it. Nobody watched three movies a day (along with the DVD extras) or sat through endless reruns or played six hours of video games at a time. And you definitely couldn't take entertainment with you in the car or on your iPod.

Don't get me wrong. I'm not complaining. I love the stuff that's available to us now. I think it's awesome that we have so many media choices, not to mention the fact that we can decide how, when, and where to consume it. But the sheer number of options has created a new problem for your generation. Even if everything you're watching is "okay" between you and God, you (and I) can still end up watching, hearing, and playing way more than we can process in a wise way.

Part of the problem is there's just so much "good" stuff out there to see and hear and play. (Your parents might disagree with me.) I can really get caught up in wanting to experience it all—every new band, every exciting TV show, every cool movie, all the latest video games. But guess what? I can't do it—and it's not just because I don't have the money. It's because there would be no time left over to do anything else with my life.

Too many students (and adults) seem to use every moment of their free time to consume media of one kind or another. Yes, they have to work and go to school and church and things like that. But the rest of their time is spent consuming media. Why? Because it's there. And it's cool.

That's a problem. Even if all media were helpful in our relationship with God, it wouldn't be helpful to try to consume it all. We have to say no to some of it simply because we need to focus our lives on more worthwhile pursuits. Saying "no" is a way of exercising self-control. The good news is that when we say no to some media options, we increase the value (and fun) of those we do choose.

Try this: In a notebook (or on your computer), track for one week every little bit of media you consume. For each day, write down the amount of time you spend doing each of the following:

· Watching TV
· Surfing the Web

- Watching movies
- Reading books
- Reading magazines
- Listening to music
- Playing video games

Next to each category, write down the shows, movies, games, books, magazines, or music you ingest. At the end of the week, add up all the time you spent on each category—and on media as a whole.

# CHAPTER 9

## HOW SHOULD I PROCESS
## ALL OF THESE STORIES?

**N**ow that we've addressed the question of whether or not we should consume media, we're going to wrap up this book by focusing on one of my favorite questions: *How can we think wisely about the media we do consume?*

Before diving in, I have to confess a personal pet peeve of mine: People who say they just want to enjoy movies, music, and TV without thinking about them. You know what? That's a lousy way to experience anything in life—especially storytelling. Not only is it lazy, but it's also impossible!

You're incapable of turning off your "message receptors." Your brain has to process every message that comes at you—every commercial, every three-minute pop song, every movie, and every gossip article you read online. Your brain has to make choices about how much credibility to give those messages and how to respond to them. Even when you don't realize it, those messages still register and get filed away in your head. If they didn't, then advertisers would stop spending a fortune to throw them at you.

Remember, we're talking about what to do with all the stories we take in. Here's a fact: Every story teaches something. Every story makes assumptions about the universe. Every story is full of ideas about what's true and what's false. If you don't participate in filtering the stories (movies, books, TV, music, games) as they come into your brain, then you give the storytellers the power to influence you with their version of the truth.

As a Jesus-follower, that should bother you. Why? Because you believe in some absolute truths about life, the universe, and everything. You've got a stake in whether those ideas are true or false, whether God is respected or dismissed, whether his version of reality is supported or mocked.

I'm not saying you should never listen to any storytellers who disagree with your biblical view of the world. If you did that, then you couldn't participate in our culture at all. But we started reviewing movies on PlanetWisdom.com because we noticed that many Christian teens were just swallowing movies whole—agreeing with the storytellers who made them, even when the messages contradicted what the Bible teaches. We want to help Christian teenagers to at least *recognize* the messages in their entertainment and be able to compare and contrast those with what we believe the Bible teaches.

Here are the questions we use while observing storytellers spin their yarns in movies, shows, music, and video games. See if they make sense to you.

- What does the story assume to be true about the world?

- What does the story teach to be true?

- What can I learn from this story's perspective? In what ways is this perspective helpful in giving me a better understanding of life?

- What assumptions or perspectives do I disagree with because of my own personal opinions and ideas?

- What assumptions or teachings should I reject because they contradict what I believe is absolute biblical truth?

These questions reveal that my approach to art and storytelling is similar to—yet also very different from—that of our secular culture. I join the culture in celebrating art as a way to come to a better understanding of the perspective of the artist—and therefore a more complete understanding of life. On the other hand, I also believe an artist can capture the reality of our world exactly—or be dead wrong in her perspective on the big issues of life. Because I've submitted my thinking to God's absolute truth, it impacts how I weigh all of the stories that flow my way.

And what are the big issues of life that always seem to pop up in our stories? A few examples:

· Who is God?

· What is normal and healthy sexuality? What are the consequences of misusing it?

· How should children respond to their parents?

· Is revenge ever justified? Why or why not?

· Are people ultimately responsible for their choices?

- Is it possible to find contentment and satisfaction outside of a relationship with God?

- Where does supernatural power come from?

- What are the origins of human life, and how does that matter?

Let's look at each of these worldview questions one at a time.

## WHAT DOES THE STORY ASSUME TO BE TRUE ABOUT THE WORLD?

Some stories make their loudest statements about life without explicitly saying anything. For instance, many sitcoms like *Friends, Seinfeld, Two and a Half Men,* and *How I Met Your Mother* make the assumption that sex between any two interested people is usually fine and that sex between two dating people who really like each other is absolutely normal. That's an assumption

about the way the world should work when it comes to sex.

Many stories also make huge assumptions about God—without ever saying his name—simply by having its characters ignore or embrace him.

When people create stories, one of the easiest things to do is write God out of existence. Whether you're watching *The Brady Bunch* or *Kill Bill,* the question *Where is God?* should always be in the back of your mind.

God is everywhere in the world. I see him as the Creator of every good thing. I can't look out the window or gaze into the sky without seeing something God made. There are also invisible creations—God's angels and those who have fallen (we call them demons)—and they interact in the affairs of people too.

Not only that, but I also see God in history. God has been active in human events since he made us. Much of the conflict that exists in the Middle East today has its beginning in the book of Genesis, where God promised Abraham that God would bless the nations of the world through the nation of Israel. And indeed he did! Christ came to us through the Jewish people. What greater blessing has the world received than that?

God came to live among us as Jesus, died for our sins, and then rose again. He began the church, and he promised to return. Early followers of Christ wrote down historical facts and the teachings of Jesus that help us stay close to God. Now he lives in believers as the Holy Spirit, and he's involved in our everyday lives.

I know that everything I have comes from God and that he supplies the food

I eat. So I pray to thank him for my meals. I also pray often for his guidance in my life.

So when I'm looking at a story, I ask, *Where is God?*

In *The Brady Bunch,* Mike Brady doesn't pray for wisdom when confronting Greg about an important matter. When Jan is concerned that everything's all about "Marcia, Marcia, Marcia!" Mike doesn't share passages of Scripture about how much God loves her and made her to be special. The Bradys rarely give thanks to God for the food he's given them or for the help they received while stranded at the bottom of the Grand Canyon. In fact, God doesn't seem to be anywhere in that television series. The writers left him out, creating the false impression that he's not an essential part of normal existence.

## WHAT DOES THE STORY TEACH TO BE TRUE?

While it's possible to recognize a story-teller's worldview from what the story *doesn't* say, we can see it more clearly in what the story does say and how it supports its ideas through the events of the story.

For instance, the *Star Wars* movies clearly taught that giving in to anger might make you powerful, but it always leads to darkness and destruction. Yoda stated that philosophy several times throughout the six films. And as the story unfolded, it showed the tragic consequences of holding on to anger, refusing to forgive, and taking revenge.

*Spider-Man 3* delivered a similar message, both in its dialogue and plot. Peter Parker, under the influence of the alien symbiote Venom, is given the opportunity to excerise his "darker side."

Parker enjoys the feeling of not exercising the virtues of self-control, mercy, and forgiveness; but ultimately he realizes that living that way leads to self-destruction.

The funny but crude *My Name Is Earl* television show proclaims its support for the spiritual idea of karma. The show's creator is on the record as stating he actually believes in karma. And his show supports the idea—both in what its characters say and in how its storylines unfold.

## WHAT CAN I LEARN FROM THIS STORY'S PERSPECTIVE?

Nearly every decently told story offers us a better understanding of life—in one way or another. I love listening to songs that tell a little story about a person's life. Oftentimes a good song succeeds because it offers a unique way of looking at the world.

Movies can do the same thing. The Farrelly Brothers are famous for their extremely crude comedies: *There's Something About Mary, Shallow Hal,* and *Stuck on You,* to name just a few. I don't recommend watching those films, necessarily. But I do admire one thing the Farrellys have done: They include people in their films who are different—physically or mentally challenged, obese, outside of society's norm in some way—and they acknowledge their differences while treating the characters as fully formed human beings who might be good, bad, crude, or kind. In doing so they've expanded their audience's perspective on how "different" people should be seen, loved, and accepted in our culture.

## WHAT ASSUMPTIONS OR PERSPECTIVES DO I DISAGREE WITH BECAUSE OF MY OWN PERSONAL OPINIONS AND IDEAS?

Sometimes we might disagree with a storyteller's worldview simply because we have a different opinion. But not every issue is a biblical worldview issue. Even among Christians there are wildly different ideas about politics, the environment, and the value of the *High School Musical* series.

It's okay to disagree with a film's take on life without making it about scriptural truth. In fact, one of the real values of art is to generate great conversation and debate about big ideas. Even if a story only convinces us of the wrongness of another perspective, it's still a helpful process.

## WHAT ASSUMPTIONS OR TEACHINGS SHOULD I REJECT BECAUSE THEY CONTRADICT WHAT I BELIEVE IS ABSOLUTE BIBLICAL TRUTH?

This is the area we focus on most often in the worldview section of our reviews on PlanetWisdom.com. I believe Christian students who see movies, listen to popular music, and watch TV should be able to understand the claims of the stories they absorb and state out loud where these stories agree and disagree with God's story, as presented in the Bible.

You can probably think of songs that suggest relationships should end when the feelings of love are gone. You've probably watched TV shows that assume evolution is responsible for all life in the universe and offer no mention of a Creator God. You've likely seen more than a few movies that suggest forgiveness has its limits and revenge is justifiable.

Instead of my listing example after example, why don't you come up with a few of your own?

List the two or three most recent story-oriented songs, TV shows, and movies you've taken in. If you're a gamer, then throw in one of those as well. Now think about the story told in each one. What are the basic elements of that story's worldview? For instance, what does the story teach or assume about God, sex, love, happiness, or any of the other big issues discussed in this book?

Now think through the other questions. What helpful perspectives does the story offer? How can it expand your understanding of life? What ideas do you disagree with in the story? What ideas clearly contradict what you believe the Bible teaches to be true?

If you had the opportunity to talk to the storyteller about the story, what would you congratulate him about? What questions would you ask? What issues would you disagree with and want to talk about?

What did you think of that exercise? Was it too hard? Was it worth the effort? It certainly adds a little work to watching, listening, reading, and playing, doesn't it? But as a Jesus-follower, you're involved in an ongoing conversation with the world around you. Listening to others' stories—even in the media—requires you to pay attention. And if you're paying attention, then you should not only learn from other points of view, but also notice when storytellers make assumptions or claims that don't ring true from a biblical perspective.

Being able to do that allows you to jump into conversation with the other media consumers around you. It gives you the opportunity to use stories as a way to point to the Greatest Story Ever Told. Talking about what fits and what falls apart within a story becomes a way to hold out the Word of Life as the answer to the deepest longing of every heart—the need to be forgiven, loved, accepted in community, made complete, and to find the ultimate happy ending.

# APPENDIX

## IDENTIFYING WORLDVIEWS

**H**ere's a chance for you to put the principles we've talked about in this book to practical use. Let's use five popular movies from the past few years to practice examining a story's worldview:

- *Juno*
- *Harry Potter and the Order of the Phoenix*
- *Bruce Almighty*
- *Star Wars: Episode III—Revenge of the Sith*
- *Spider-Man 3*

We reviewed each of these films at PlanetWisdom.com. I've included those reviews, as well as the discussion of each film's worldview, in the pages that follow. Before you read what we wrote, though, take time to answer some questions and make your own determination.

Keep two things in mind as you read the following reviews. First, our reviews don't necessarily address the question of whether or not you should see a film. Instead they focus on how Christians—those of us who treat God's Word as actual truth—should think about the messages of the story.

Second, it's okay to separate the question of whether or not we "like" a movie from a discussion of how that story deals with issues of truth. For example, I might have loved the writing, acting, and directing in *Juno* without liking its messages. Or I might have agreed strongly with some of the messages in *Evan Almighty* without liking the film as art. That's why we make the decision on the PlanetWisdom.com reviews to separate the "Verdict" section from the "Worldview" section.

Okay, let's take a crack at examining your own response to the worldviews of the following films, based on your understanding of God's worldview from the Bible.

## *JUNO*: YOUR ANALYSIS

Before reading our take on the film from PlanetWisdom.com, take a minute to think through your own response to it from a Christian perspective. Jot down a few of your ideas. You don't have to answer every question; zero in on the ones that fit this film.

What did you think of the movie on its own terms? Did you like it? Love it? What did you think of the writing, acting, directing, and soundtrack? How would you evaluate the film as art?

What are the basic elements of the story's worldview? For instance, what does the story teach or assume about God, sex, love, happiness or any of the other big issues discussed in this book?

What helpful perspectives does the story offer? How can it expand your understanding of life? What ideas do you disagree with in the story? What ideas clearly contradict what you believe the Bible teaches to be true?

If you had the opportunity to talk to the storytellers about the story, what would you congratulate them about? What questions would you ask? What issues would you disagree with and want to talk about?

## *JUNO*: THE PLANETWISDOM.COM REVIEW

### THE STORY

Juno (Ellen Page) is 16 and pregnant by best-friend-not-a-boyfriend-so-much Paulie Bleeker (Michael Cera). She claims she had sex because she was bored. He claims she totally wanted to. Everyone seems to agree it wasn't his decision. Juno reveals the secret to her equally quick-talking best friend Leah (Olivia Thirby), who asks which abortion clinic Juno will use. And Juno does go to one—only to change her mind when she gets creeped out by the weird vibe of the place (and an odd pro-life friend's declaration that "Your baby has fingernails.")

Juno tells her dad (J.K. Simmons) and step-mom (Allison Janney) that she's pregnant and that she's going to have the baby and put it up for adoption. Her parents are disappointed in her "stupid" choice to have (unprotected) sex, but they also matter-of-factly support her.

Juno picks an adoptive couple out of the Penny Saver newspaper and goes to see them with her dad. Vanessa (Jennifer Garner) and Mark (Jason Bateman) have been trying to have a child for five years. They live in a McMansion in the suburbs, where Mark works from home as a cool-for-his-age musician.

Juno struggles through her pregnancy, never losing her resolve to give up the baby while building an odd relationship with Vanessa and Mark—and working out her relationship with Bleeker, the baby's father.

## THE VERDICT

As a story, *Juno* gets better as it rolls along. For the first 20 minutes or so, everything about it screams "overdone quirky indie film." The script (by former stripper Diablo Cody) is so crammed with fast-paced "teen speak" and quirky asides that it moves past cool to just plain silly for the first few scenes. The eventually decent, earnest singer-songwriter soundtrack blares over montages and meaningful moments in a way that practically begs for indie cred. "Look how cool these songs are!"

But then it all starts to settle down as we get to know and like the characters. Director Ivan Reitman stops trying to be so now(!) and gets into telling the story. And it's a good story. The characters never stop being Characters, but the choices they struggle with and make feel completely real—not always good or healthy, but always genuine and human.

The cast is universally pretty good, especially Ellen Page, Michael Cera, and Jason Bateman.

And the final act delivers both a few surprises and some unexpectedly powerful emotions.

In short, it's a well-made, funny, real-feeling indie film. Still, the experience as a whole left me uneasy. It's supposed to be life-affirming, I think, but the conclusions of the movie's worldview landed in my soul with a troubling thud. More on that later.

Also, Juno and her friends swear and talk really crudely about all things sexual as naturally as truck drivers or construction workers or other hairy middle-aged tough guys. Actually, they do so more naturally, as if "that's just how teens talk now." And maybe it is in some cases. But it's enough to earn the film's PG-13 rating.

## WORLDVIEW
*[Warning: Spoilers ahead. To dig into the film's worldview, I'll have to talk about some key plot points. Turn back now if you don't want to know.]*

On the positive side, Juno instinctively rejects getting an abortion. It's not a bold pro-life statement, necessarily. Abortion isn't condemned. It just feels wrong to Juno. In fact, most of Juno's choices about her pregnancy are positive and mature and life-valuing. She makes crude jokes about the baby and the pregnancy, but she also radically changes her diet to keep the child healthy. She cares deeply about finding it a good home. She owns the consequences of her choice to have sex and makes the best of it.

On the other hand, the film seems to exist in a moral vacuum. Nothing is presented as right or wrong for any reason, and nobody seems to wrestle over the morality of any choice. Was it wrong for Juno to have sex before marriage? Nobody seems to think so. Would it have been wrong for her to get an abortion—or for her not to get one? It's clear she'd be supported either way. Is her final decision about the adoption healthy or un-healthy for her baby? Writer Cody and direc-tor Reitman leave all those sticky questions up to the audience, which is fine. But the re-sult is that Juno and her family and friends seem to live in a world beyond morality—and certainly beyond God's view of morality.

The saddest worldview issue for me, however, has to do with the men in Juno's life. And I don't honestly blame the creative team too much for this one, because it reflects more and more of the men in the real world. None of those guys is able to take the lead or accept the responsibility for his choices.

Bleeker, the baby's shy, easygoing father, is told by everyone that having sex wasn't his choice. Guys can't help themselves, I guess. They'll have sex if given the opportunity. In the same way, Bleeker never asks for any role in deciding the fate of his baby. No leadership. No responsibility.

Mark, the adoptive dad, makes a commitment to raise the baby. He signs his name to the documents. He makes an agreement with his wife and with Juno. And then he bails. No leadership. No responsibility. No commitment.

Juno's dad is a great guy who cares for his daughter. But is a dad who doesn't teach his kids the difference between right and wrong a good man? Is a dad's only job to be supportive when his kids get into trouble? Or should he step in early on to give some direction based on a moral worldview?

The closest he comes to that ideal is when Juno asks him if any relationship between a man and woman can survive for life. He admits it's always hard, but then describes an unconditional "liking" between two people that at first sounds a lot like biblical love. The problem is that it's all about someone "being crazy about you" even when you're unattractive. The relationships that work "forever" are the ones in which someone is unconditionally committed to you even when they're not crazy about you—because those crazy feelings can fade and re-emerge often in a marriage. It's the kind of love God tells men to give their wives.

Cody, Reitman, and company don't have any real men to inject into the story, so they leave us only with the "true love" of a couple of likable wise-beyond-their-years 16 year-olds, embarking on another not-so-wise romance-without-commitment relationship.

## HARRY POTTER AND THE ORDER OF THE PHOENIX: YOUR ANALYSIS

Before reading our take on the film from PlanetWisdom.com, take a minute to think through your own response to it from a Christian perspective. Jot down a few of your ideas. You don't have to answer every question; zero in on the ones that fit this film.

What did you think of the movie on its own terms? Did you like it? Love it? What did you think of the writing, acting, directing, and soundtrack? How would you evaluate the film as art?

What are the basic elements of the story's worldview? For instance, what does the story teach or assume about God, sex, love, happiness or any of the other big issues discussed in this book?

What helpful perspectives does the story offer? How can it expand your understanding of life? What ideas do you disagree with in the story? What ideas clearly contradict what you believe the Bible teaches to be true?

If you had the opportunity to talk to the storytellers about the story, what would you congratulate them about? What questions would you ask? What issues would you disagree with and want to talk about?

## HARRY POTTER AND THE ORDER OF THE PHOENIX: THE PLANETWISDOM.COM REVIEW

### THE STORY

In the summer after Harry's run-in with the alive-again evil Lord Voldemort (Ralph Fiennes), in which a boy was killed and Harry barely escaped, a smear campaign has been launched against him and Headmaster Dumbledore (Michael Gambon). The head of the Ministry of Magic refuses to believe Voldemort is alive, calling Harry a liar, even when he is attacked in the non-magical world by a pair of Dementors. Harry returns to Hogwarts School of Witchcraft and Wizardry under heavy suspicion.

He has the backing of a group called the Order of the Phoenix, which includes Harry's "godfather" Sirius Black (Gary Oldman), Professor Snape (Alan Rickman), former professor Mad-Eye Moody, and former Professor Lupin. But once at school, only his friends Ron (Rupert Grint), Hermione (Emma Watson), and a few other students can help Harry with his growing sense of "connection" (especially in disturbing dreams) to Lord Voldemort.

To make matters worse, the Ministry of Magic has assigned a new Defense Against the Dark Arts teacher, Dolores Umbridge (Imelda Staunton), to return order to the school by keeping the students from practicing any magic and restricting all of their movements. Umbridge rules with an iron fist, driving out several professors, and using cruel punishments with the students, especially Harry, who refuses to stop proclaiming that Voldemort has returned. Since the school won't do it, Harry begins secretly training his fellow students for battle by teaching them defense spells and techniques. The preparations for the "war" with Voldemort's growing army have definitely begun.

### THE VERDICT

If you've read the massive book or seen the nearly two-and-a-half-hour film, you'll notice that my summation is woefully short of detail. It's the same challenge faced by new-to-the-series writer Michael Goldenberg and director David Yates. You've got to leave a lot of the book on the cutting room floor when you make a *Harry Potter* movie. That reality has left several of the films up to this point feeling a little patchworky and meandering to me, as the creative teams tried to include all they could without sacrificing the main thrust of the storytelling.

Honestly, I think Goldenberg and Yates succeed better than the others in keeping this episode of the Potter franchise focused on a single thread. Of course, the film ends without full resolution—and several events still feel undeveloped—but these guys deliver a more satisfying beginning, middle, and end than the last couple of *HP* films did.

It's true that things move a little more slowly this time around. We get fewer "wow-factor," large-scale effects sequences—and far less comic relief and teen angst. Instead, "Phoenix" is really about just three major plot lines, all of which are serious, relevant, and mostly resolved.

The performers, young and old alike, all improve with each new film. Daniel Radcliffe, Emma Watson, and Rupert Grint have become truly decent actors, and the all-star cast of adult acting heavyweights are great fun to watch. I especially liked the pink-clad, iron-fisted Imelda Staunton as Dolores Umbridge. And, as always, I wouldn't want to be left alone in a room with Alan Rickman's Professor Snape.

The story's ever-darker tone has more to do with its emphasis on "serious times" than it does with "darker magic." Yes, there's plenty of playing-with-fire spell-casting and wand flourishing going on here, but the central focus has fully shifted to the conflict between good and evil. Harry's story is no longer about the "wonder of magic"; it's about using magic in a life-and-death struggle to stand for what's right (or wrong, if you're a villain). And that worked for me, in spite of the long running time and less "fun" storytelling.

This is the second PG-13 rated *HP* movie, due to more scary stuff, more dark themes, and a little language.

## WORLDVIEW

As with the other *HP* movies, *Phoenix* presents several interesting worldviews. I'll tackle two.

The Ministry of Magic, which rules the world of law-abiding magicians, wizards, and witches cannot accept the reality that great evil is at work in the world. The leader of this body and those under him commit serious crimes against Harry, Dumbledore, and others to suppress that truth. Their intentions are apparently good—to stop the spread of panic, to keep people from being manipulated by needless fear, to maintain orderliness. But refusing to acknowledge the reality of evil often makes that evil stronger.

Surveys reveal that fewer and fewer people believe in the existence of real spiritual evil in the form of Satan and demons. The Bible warns Christians to take the threat of a supernatural enemy with deadly seriousness, describing Satan as a vicious, hungry beast looking to destroy us (1 Peter 5:8). And Paul urges his readers to learn to defend themselves against spiritual evil by putting on spiritual armor and taking up spiritual weapons (Ephesians 6).

Some people mock the idea of Satan and demons, but we can't take those forces lightly. It's true that God has won the war, but he calls us to step up and participate in the battle by being self-controlled, alert, and focused on a life that matters.

I was less impressed with the film's all-too-common worldview idea that all of us have good and evil inside of us, but we have the power to choose which path to follow. Sirius Black says as much to Harry when Potter confesses his struggle to overcome anger and dark thoughts. The Bible is clear that none of us comes with true goodness built into us. Our sin nature kills it. We must truly be redeemed by the blood of Jesus through faith in Jesus to gain access to God's goodness (righteousness) (Philippians 3:8-9).

As with most secular stories about the internal battle between good and evil, *Phoenix* suggests the answer lies within ourselves (as well as in friendship). That stops short of

Scripture's teaching that we need to be made alive and transformed from without, by God's power, before we can hope to win the battle with our own darkness.

*NOTE: No matter what anybody says about the* Harry Potter *series, remember that whether or not you take part in it is between you (and your parents) and God. Just because others are okay with it doesn't mean you have to be—and the same applies in reverse. Honor your conscience and the Holy Spirit's leading in your life as to what you put into your mind.*

### *BRUCE ALMIGHTY:* YOUR ANALYSIS

Before reading our take on the film from PlanetWisdom.com, take a minute to think through your own response to it from a Christian perspective. Jot down a few of your ideas. You don't have to answer every question; zero in on the ones that fit this film.

What did you think of the movie on its own terms? Did you like it? Love it? What did you think of the writing, acting, directing, and soundtrack? How would you evaluate the film as art?

What are the basic elements of the story's worldview? For instance, what does the story teach or assume about God, sex, love, happiness or any of the other big issues discussed in this book?

What helpful perspectives does the story offer? How can it expand your understanding of life? What ideas do you disagree with in the story? What ideas clearly contradict what you believe the Bible teaches to be true?

If you had the opportunity to talk to the storytellers about the story, what would you congratulate them about? What questions would you ask? What issues would you disagree with and want to talk about?

## BRUCE ALMIGHTY: THE PLANETWISDOM.COM REVIEW

### THE STORY

Jim Carrey stars as Bruce Nolan, a TV news reporter who specializes in silly, sappy community stories. When the anchor position he's longed for goes to someone else, Bruce comes unglued. He sees every bad thing in his life as evidence that God is not doing his job. After alienating his live-in girlfriend Grace (Jennifer Aniston) with his self-pity, he loudly challenges God to show himself.

Bruce ends up following a mysterious lead to a warehouse labeled Omni Presents, Inc. He meets a man (Morgan Freeman) who eventually reveals himself to be God and who gives Bruce all his powers—to give Bruce a chance to do God's work better than God does. With all that power, will Bruce be able to make his own life better? Will he be able to save his relationship with Grace? And what about all those people who are praying for God's help?

### THE VERDICT

However thoughtful the subject matter here, *Bruce Almighty* is not intended to be part drama, as *The Truman Show* and *The Majestic* were. It's definitely meant to be silly/funny, in the spirit of *Liar, Liar.* It includes Carrey's trademark rubber face-making, body-warping movements, and a couple of brand-new catch phrases (this year's "Allllrighty then").

While that manic Carrey goofiness does provide some big laughs, the energy level is toned down from the days of *Dumb and Dumber* and *Ace Ventura: Pet Detective.* He's most funny when he's drunk with his newfound power, using it to get revenge on his enemies, seduce Grace, and make himself look good.

Unless you look at *Bruce Almighty* as an illustration of how dangerous a mere human with God's power would be, it can definitely come across as offensive to the true God. I cringed when Bruce parted his red soup, walked on water, and called himself the Alpha and Omega. But the point of the story is that even with those powers, a human would make a lousy God. Only God can handle God's power wisely. (More on that later.)

Morgan Freeman remains mostly understated as God. Thankfully, the movie doesn't call for him to talk in a booming voice or explain all his actions. Instead, Freeman plays the version of God that he shows to Bruce as an effortless and confident being who holds Bruce accountable for his words and actions, but is also ready to help him grow.

As Grace, Jennifer Aniston plays the sincere and concerned girlfriend, but little else.

Nearly as funny as Carrey, Steven Carell gets far too little screen time as the jerk who gets the anchor job over Bruce. The scene where Bruce messes with Carell's ability to talk on air might be the most laugh-out-loud funny in the whole film. (Be sure to stick around for the outtakes during the credits for more.)

*Bruce Almighty* earns its PG-13 rating with bad language, crude humor, and the pre-sex scene between Bruce and Grace that's played for laughs but includes some erotic behavior between the unmarried couple.

## WORLDVIEW

*[Warning: Spoilers ahead. To dig into the film's worldview, I'll have to talk about some key plot points. Turn back now if you don't want to know.]*

The movie's presentation of God and how humans can and should relate to him provides several positive principles for biblical Christians. And even where it falls short of truth, *Bruce Almighty* provides an excellent opportunity to talk about God with non-Christian friends.

First, the positive things.

1. Bruce's initial belief is that it's God's job to make sure our lives are mostly happy and working well. Instead of taking responsibility for his own actions, Bruce blames God for everything he doesn't like and gives God credit for nothing good in his life (James 1:17). Over the course of the film, however, Bruce learns that God's goal is not to make sure everyone is happy and getting what they want (James 4:1-10). He also learns that we bring many of life's worst things on ourselves through our selfishness.

2. As mentioned earlier, the movie demonstrates that even with all of God's power, we would not make good gods. I wouldn't want to live in a world in which I had power over everything, because I'm not, by nature, all good or all loving. Only God can be trusted with God's power because only he is completely and unswervingly good.

3. Though some Christians may put this in the negative category, the movie shows that

God doesn't force humans to love him. Bruce learns that though he can use his power to do a lot for Grace, he can't make her love him. She has to come to that on her own. God, of course, can do whatever he wants. But humans are ultimately held accountable for whether we accept or reject him.

4. Amazingly for a Hollywood film, Bruce even comes to a place of sincere repentance. On his knees, he says something like, "I don't want this anymore. I can't do it on my own. I want you to decide what's right and wrong for me. I surrender to you." This is almost the definition of biblical repentance—turning from my way of living to God's way for me and trusting him to do as he pleases with me. What a shocking and refreshing thing to see in a movie.

Now, the negative things.

1. As with most Hollywood depictions of God and his work, Jesus is never mentioned in the movie (except as a swear word). However, the Bible teaches that there's no way to have a relationship with God except through Jesus (John 14:6). We believe that surrendering to your own understanding of God is pointless

without coming to him through Jesus for the forgiveness of our sins and eternity with the Father. Without Jesus, there's no real power to live the way God wants us to.

2. At one point, God says something like, "Most humans spend too much time looking up for help." What Bruce learns from that is that humans need to focus on "making our own miracles" through right living and helping others. The Bible teaches exactly the opposite.

God's goal for every Christian is that we become like Jesus. If you've read the book of John, you've probably noticed that nearly every time Jesus talks, he says his words and actions are from the Father. He is totally dependent on the Father. James writes that God uses hard times in our lives to get us to depend on him more, not less. Total dependence equals total maturity (James 1:2-4).

Yes, God wants us to live right and love others, but he wants us to do it in his power and with his help (Galatians 5:22-23). Unlike the movie version of God, our real heavenly Father doesn't want us to learn to handle things on our own. Our strength to do right comes from him, through Jesus.

If you're a Christian and you see or talk about this movie with friends, take the opportunity to ask what they believe about God and to share your own understanding of what the Bible teaches about a relationship with him through Jesus. *Bruce Almighty* might give you a great opportunity to start a conversation that could take your relationship to a whole new level.

## *STAR WARS: EPISODE III—REVENGE OF THE SITH*: YOUR ANALYSIS

Before reading our take on the film from PlanetWisdom.com, take a minute to think through your own response to it from a Christian perspective. Jot down a few of your ideas. You don't have to answer every question; zero in on the ones that fit this film.

What did you think of the movie on its own terms? Did you like it? Love it? What did you think of the writing, acting, directing, and soundtrack? How would you evaluate the film as art?

What are the basic elements of the story's

worldview? For instance, what does the story teach or assume about God, sex, love, happiness or any of the other big issues discussed in this book?

What helpful perspectives does the story offer? How can it expand your understanding of life? What ideas do you disagree with in the story? What ideas clearly contradict what you believe the Bible teaches to be true?

If you had the opportunity to talk to the storytellers about the story, what would you congratulate them about? What questions would you ask? What issues would you disagree with and want to talk about?

## *STAR WARS: EPISODE III—REVENGE OF THE SITH*: THE PLANETWISDOM.COM REVIEW

### THE STORY

It's been three years since the end of *Star Wars: Episode II—Attack of the Clones*. Aided by R2-D2, Anakin Skywalker (Hayden Christensen), and Obi-Wan Kenobi (Ewan McGregor) still fight side by side to overcome

Count Dooku (Christopher Lee), General Grievous, and the droid armies. But with the war nearing its end, the Jedi Council and Chancellor Palpatine seem to be growing distrustful of each other.

Led by Yoda and Mace Windu (Samuel L. Jackson), the Council suspects Palpatine might not give up his position and return power to the Senate once the droids are defeated. Anakin, who sees Palpatine as a mentor, feels caught between his loyalty to the Jedis and his loyalty to the Chancellor.

At the same time, Anakin learns that his secret marriage to Padmé has resulted in a pregnancy. His joy sours when he begins having visions that she will die in childbirth. When Palpatine suggests to him that it might be possible to use the dark side of the Force to save her, Anakin falls into conflict. He's torn between saving Padmé and following the Jedi code. Eventually, he must decide.

### THE VERDICT

Wow. Twenty-two years after the release of *Return of the Jedi,* the "Star Wars" saga finally returns to its former glory. It's hard to express just how much better *Revenge of the Sith* is than the previous two shrug-inducing episodes. From the acting and writing to the computer-generated effects to the storytelling and pace, *Sith* is more than just improved. It's actually really good—and a satisfying conclusion to the tarnished series.

To start with, the movie looks amazing. Space battles between hundreds of individual ships demand to be watched again to catch missed moments. Real and digital sets are gigantically scaled with a retro-futuristic feeling of 1930's New York architecture. The weapons, creatures, vehicles, and whole worlds show off impressive imagination and painstaking detail. And even five lightsaber showdowns somehow avoid becoming tedious, maintaining the suspense.

Mostly a relentless action movie, *Sith* succeeds because of the story. All the actors are solid, even the digital ones. They play their parts big, but the movie is big enough to hold them. Somehow, you accept the fact that you're watching a space "opera" play out larger-than-life themes with characters that have been part of our culture for a generation.

In fact, the film does something very few movies can get away with these days. It presents a genuine tragedy. We've always known exactly where the story was headed, but it was hard to picture how the boy from *Episode I* could become the evil Lord Vader. The transformation is believable and truly sad.

Not everything worked for me. Some of the humor, especially early on, felt forced. R2 and the battle droids are given a little bit of a *Loony Toons* quality with their comments and movements. Ewan McGregor sometimes comes across as uncomfortable in Obi-Wan's tunic. But Hayden Christensen nails the wounded, angry, untrusting Anakin this time around. It's no easy task to make the villain into the most sympathetic character on screen.

The film's rating gets bumped up to PG-13 due to much-increased and graphic violence. Heads, limbs, and torsos—both human and droid—get bloodlessly carved up by lightsabers. The body count includes several small children. And one character is shown in agony, burned and mutilated. This is hardly a kids' movie.

## WORLDVIEW

From a Christian perspective, *Episode III* offers both a powerful illustration of the choices that can lead us toward destruction—and some blatantly unbiblical teachings on issues of spirituality and life after death.

Let's start with the negative. As with all the *Star Wars* films, writer George Lucas embeds in the religion of the Jedi some of the principles of Eastern philosophy and belief systems. In counseling Anakin, Yoda says that death is just part of life, that death simply causes a person to "transform in the Force." We know from other films that the Force is a kind of life energy that exists everywhere, that contains both a light and a dark side, and that must be kept "in balance."

By contrast, Christians are convinced that God is everywhere, but that he is a person and only good. He has no dark side, and he doesn't need to be balanced. Evil is not equal or opposite to God's goodness. It is a corruption of it. Evil is defined as a resistance to God's goodness and the resulting separation from him that it causes. Christians also understand that life on this earth is followed not by becoming part of God or some universal energy, but by each individual receiving from God reward or punishment based on faith in Jesus.

Yoda further says that the key to finding freedom in life is to give up all desire, to let go of anything you fear to lose. It's a common Buddhist teaching. The Bible also teaches that wrong desires and the fear of losing what we want is destructive. (See James 4:1-3.) Instead of just "letting go" of those desires, though, we're urged to find peace by giving them to God and trusting him to provide for us out of his fierce and personal love for us. (Check out James 4:4-10.) That's the path to real peace. (See Philippians 4:4-7.)

One other comment in *Sith* stands out in contrast to what the Bible teaches. When Anakin tells Obi-Wan, "If you're not with me, you're my enemy," Obi-Wan responds by saying that absolutes are "the way of the Sith." In other words, absolutes are evil. That's confusing, because the Jedi seem to stand for some pretty firm absolutes throughout the story. It also feels like a jab at anyone who believes in absolute truth about God and his relationship with humans.

On the positive side, Anakin's choice to compromise all of his other principles in order to get the power to save his wife is a great example of the path many of us follow to major and minor destruction. Who wouldn't want to save the love of his life? I would. But Anakin wants to cheat death for his own gain, because he "can't live without her."

How many of us have made wrong choices out of the fear of losing a relationship or not being popular or missing out on some exciting experience? And who hasn't experienced something negative after compromising what we knew was right?

Ultimately, too many people follow their fears of losing what seems most important in life into a destruction far worse than what Anakin experiences. Jesus said it this way: "Whoever finds his life will lose it, and whoever loses his life for my sake will find it" (Matthew 10:39, NIV). It takes courage to risk it all to follow Jesus. But in the end, it always costs more not to follow him.

## *SPIDER-MAN 3*: YOUR ANALYSIS

Before reading our take on the film from PlanetWisdom.com, take a minute to think through your own response to it from a Christian perspective. Jot down a few of your ideas. You don't have to answer every question; zero in on the ones that fit this film.

What did you think of the movie on its own terms? Did you like it? Love it? What did you think of the writing, acting, directing, and soundtrack? How would you evaluate the film as art?

What are the basic elements of the story's worldview? For instance, what does the story teach or assume about God, sex, love, happiness or any of the other big issues discussed in this book?

What helpful perspectives does the story offer? How can it expand your understanding of life? What ideas do you disagree with in the story? What ideas clearly contradict what you believe the Bible teaches to be true?

If you had the opportunity to talk to the storytellers about the story, what would you congratulate them about? What questions would you ask? What issues would you disagree with and want to talk about?

## SPIDER-MAN 3:
## THE PLANETWISDOM.COM REVIEW

### THE STORY

Peter Parker (Tobey Maguire) is in a pretty good place, for a change. His girl Mary Jane (Kirsten Dunst) knows his secret, and she still loves him. And she's reached her dream of singing on Broadway. Maybe more impressive, the people of NYC love Spider-Man for the crime-fighting hero he is. They're even giving him the key to the city. He's decided to be a happy guy—and maybe even to pop the big question to MJ and live happily ever after.

But that would make for a lousy movie. Instead, former best friend Harry Osborn (James Franco) comes gunning for Peter for killing his dad. And the police discover that Flint Marko (Thomas Haden Church), a criminal who just escaped from prison and stumbled into the odd power to dissolve into sand and harness it as a weapon, is the man who really killed Peter's Uncle Ben. Oh, and a new kid (Topher Grace) is trying to move in on Peter's turf as the go-to photographer for the *Daily Bugle*.

To top it off, Peter gets infected with a black, slimy substance from outer space that binds itself to a host and feeds off negative inclinations like anger, aggression, revenge, and bad hair. It forms itself into a cool black-gray version of the Spidey suit that Peter can't bring himself to take off. Cue: Evil Pete trashing his relationships and risking his rep as a good guy and a hero in order to make his enemies pay.

## THE VERDICT

If it seems from that synopsis like there's a lot going on, there is. Director Sam Raimi and his team seem to have answered the question of how to live up to the first two films by including more of everything that made them great—lots of relationship-driven character development; plenty of rock 'em, sock 'em comic book action sequences; big doses of serious worldview issues; and even several scenes of wacky comic relief. Honestly, it's just a little too much to hold together in one 160-minute story.

Don't get me wrong. I enjoyed the movie—a lot. Most of it works really well. It just doesn't come together to reach the satisfaction level of *Spider-Man 2*. The big battle sequences are good, but none of them grabbed me as forcefully as that battle on the train with Dock Ock—or that car coming through the store window—in *S-M2*. The comic relief is often funny, but it also feels a little distracting—as if Raimi doesn't trust the weight of the drama he's built out of the connections between Peter, MJ, Harry, and even the Sandman.

On the cool side, Black Spidey looks good (even though he's bad). He looks even cooler when he becomes the Venom character with the evil teeth and long, pointy claws. As a villain, he worked much better for me than the Sandman character, who's tough to hold onto, motivation-wise. Most of the performances are decent, with Maguire getting the bulk of the juicy stuff as evil Pete, complete with awkward strutting and bad emo hair (and what looked like eyeliner, at one point).

At moments like that—and when evil Pete does a sexy dance with the police chief's daughter to punish MJ for something—the movie loses focus completely and leans into the absurd, as if Raimi is purposely reminding us this is all just for fun. Interesting, but it also breaks the spell of the storytelling.

In spite of my down tone, though, it really is a good, meaty film made all the richer by the big, unsubtle messages upon which Raimi builds the whole operatic tale. (More on that later.) You don't walk out with the triumphant feeling often associated with comic book films, necessarily, but *Spidey 3* leaves you with plenty to mull over. And it left me looking forward to catching it again to put all the pieces together a little more clearly.

The movie nabs its PG-13 rating with plenty of action violence—some of it fatal—and a little blood. I only caught a few swear words, and sexual content is limited to kisses and that strange little dance number.

### WORLDVIEW

One thing I've appreciated about the whole *Spider-Man* series is Raimi's commitment to trumpeting valuable messages between the web-slinging mayhem. In the first film, Peter famously accepted the now-familiar notion

that "with great power comes great responsibility." In the second film, he wrestled with
the idea that we must all take responsibility
for the consequences of our own choices.

In S-M3, the messages are even less subtle. And
for me, at least, they're even more powerful.

Raimi takes a lot of time to build big com-
passion for everyone on screen—and for all of
us sitting in the audience. He cares that we
understand the pain felt by heroes and vil-
lains alike. Peter has been unjustly betrayed
and has lost his beloved uncle. Because of one
costly, understandable mistake, Sandman has
lost his family. MJ feels justifiably neglected.
Harry's lost his dad.

But Raimi doesn't just stop with the notion
that "everybody hurts." He goes on to say that
our suffering does not make it okay for us to
hurt others. Personal pain is not a justification
for holding on to anger, revenge, and selfishness. No matter how difficult our lives become,
hurting others is always wrong.

That's not to say it isn't fun. Peter, Harry,
and Eddie Brock (Topher Grace) all get a rush

of power from giving in to the dark side of revenge. And they like it. At one point, Brock says, "I like being mad. It makes me happy." Anger gives focus and strength—for a while. And then, like the sticky black stuff from outer space, it takes over our whole lives.

Spidey would have no argument with the Bible's teaching to rid our lives of anger, rage, and malice (Colossians 3:8). And though, in the film's most moving scene, Peter realizes his need to forgive those who have wronged him, the story only hints at the reason for such forgiveness. While an enemy prays to God for Peter's death, Peter confronts his vengeful heart in the bell tower of a church.

Aunt May later tells Peter he must learn to forgive himself, and Peter praises another character for embracing his better self. God's Word aims much higher than self-goodness. It teaches that we must accept not our own forgiveness, but God's—available only through Jesus. (See Ephesians 1:7.) It's because we've been forgiven so much that we can turn around and forgive those who hurt us. (See Ephesians 4:32.) We can look and look, but we'll never find good in ourselves